ALSO BY KEVIN YOUNG

TO REPEL GHOSTS

MOST WAY HOME

AS EDITOR

GIANT STEPS: THE NEW GENERATION
  OF AFRICAN AMERICAN WRITERS

jelly roll

jelly roll

{ A BLUES }

(composed & arranged by)

kevin young

ALFRED A. KNOPF, NEW YORK

2003

THIS IS A BORZOI BOOK
PUBLISHED BY ALFRED A. KNOPF

www.randomhouse.com/knopf/poetry

Knopf, Borzoi Books, and the colophon are registered trademarks
of Random House, Inc.

Library of Congress Cataloging-in-Publication Data
Young, Kevin.
Jelly roll : a blues / Kevin Young.—1st ed.
p. cm.
ISBN 0-375-41460-6
1. African Americans—Poetry. 2. Blues (Music)—Poetry. I. Title.
PS3575.O798 J45 2003
811'.54—dc21   2002070935
Manufactured in the United States of America
First Edition

ACKNOWLEDGMENTS

Some of these poems were originally published in the following journals:

Callaloo: Cakewalk, Cotillion, Disaster Movie Theme Music, Dixieland, Gumbo, Ramble.

Fence: Rhapsody.

Figdust: Cantata.

Georgia Review: Piano Player.

New York Times Book Review: Can-Can.

The New Yorker: Busking, Intermezzo.

Open City: Encore, Sorrow Song, Saxophone Solo, Muzak.

Pleiades: Parlor Song, Shimmy, Nocturne.

Seneca Review: Scherzo, Aubade.

TriQuarterly: Requiem.

Verse: Litany.

"Shimmy" also appeared in a limited-edition broadside from Maryland Institute, College of Art. "Epithalamion," or marriage poem, was written for the wedding of Karl and Wanda Cole-Frieman, and read at the wedding of John Yau and Eve Ascheim. May it grace yours too.

Thanks to my agent Eileen Cope for her ongoing support, Deborah Garrison for her editorial brilliance, and Ilana Kurshan for all her phrenological faculties. Thanks to the University of Georgia, Indiana University, the MacDowell Colony, and the good folks at 283 for the time and support in writing these blues. Thanks are also due to all who read and helped this book early on, particularly Elizabeth Alexander, Eisa Davis, Sean Hill, Richard Eoin Nash, Colson Whitehead, and John Yau. Very special thanks go to Kate Tuttle, the best cure for the blues anyone could hope for.

I love my baby
But my baby don't love me

I love my baby wooo
My baby don't love me

I really loves that woman
Can't stand to leave her be

A-ain't but one thing
Makes Mister Johnson drink

I gets low bout how you treat me baby
I begin to think

Oh babe
Our love won't be the same

You break my heart
When you call Mister So & So's name

{ Robert Johnson }

CONTENTS

{2}

jelly roll

EPITHALAMION

Before the world
was water, just
before the fire

or the wool,
was you—
yes—your hands

a stillness—
a mountain. Marry
me. Let the ash

invade us & the ants
the aints—
let—my God—

the anger
but do not answer
No—such stars

shooting, unresolved
are about to be ours—
if we wish. Yes—

the course, the sail
we've set—our mind—
leaves no wake

just swimming sleep.
Stand
& I will be born

from your arm—
a thing eagled, open,
above the unsettled,

moon-made sea.

★

1

Sweet silver trumpets,
Jesus!

{ **Langston Hughes** }

CAKEWALK

Baby, you make
me want

to burn up all
my pies

to give over
an apple to fire

or loose track
of time & send

a large pecan
smokeward, or

sink some peach
cobbler. See, to me

you are a Canada
someplace north

I have been, for years,
headed & not

known it.
If only I'd read

the moss on the tree!
instead of shaking

it for fruit—
you are a found

fallen thing—
a freedom—not this red

bloodhound ground—

DIXIELAND

I want the spell
of a woman—her

smell & say-so—
her humid

hands I seek—zombied—
The bayou

of my blood—standing
water & the 'squitoes

all hungry—*hongry*—
to see both our bodies

knocked out—dragged
quicksand down—

They'll put up posters—
have you seen—all over town—

Days later we'll be drug
naked from the swamp

that is us—re-
suscitated, rescued—

the cops without one clue.

SIREN

On the fire throw
another can of sterno

that hiss is
flame finding

the wood wet
or, as yet, green—

I mean, darling,
to be an ABC

extinguisher, kept
handy, kitchened, a six-alarm

APB—the loom
of the trucks

hydrants in bloom
the dalmation

with the bad back
& heart—be me—

RHYTHM & BLUES

Through the wall
I hear them

again—the couple—
not fighting

but doing
the other thing—

his cat-cries
as if a trapped beast—

even above the music
saying God—

her quiet—my own
eavesdropped breath—

SHIMMY

You are, lady,
admired—secret

something kept
afar, a near,

anywhere
mist gathers

like moss.
Here the moths

in their winning
way flash, burn,

return—
Old flame,

you are insurance,
this horse I'm betting

against—longshot,
fix, undecided pyro-

technic. You fit
my tongue like arsenic.

ZOOT

Speakeasy she.
Am sunder.

Are.
She pluck

herself, songing—
I strum. Am.

Strut, straggle,
hum. The half-

notes risen in
my throat! She flute

me, fa, fast, quick-
silvered—

ETUDE

I love making
love most just

after—adrift—
the cries & sometime

tears over, our strong
swimming done—

sheet wreck—
mattress a life-

boat, listing—

DITTY

You, rare as Georgia
snow. Falling

hard. Quick.
Candle shadow.

  The cold
spell that catches

us by surprise.
The too-early blooms,

tricked, gardenias blown about,
circling wind. Green figs.

 Nothing stays. I want
to watch you walk

the hall to the cold tile
bathroom—all

  night, a lifetime.

RAGTIME

Like hot food
I love you

like warm
bread & cold

cuts, butter
sammiches

or, days later, after
Thanksgiving

when I want
whatever's left

JINGLE

Put me on the rack
in the back

sweetie, demote
& discount me

Carry me down
to the basement, low

low prices, one
night only!

Honey I wants
to be free

with purchase,
lagniappe on

the side—a street
or commercial

break, an ache—

BOOGIE-WOOGIE

I'll be your lunch
date, your party

favorite—wind
up & watch me run

down—*ten
nine eight*—

I'm your New
Year's Eve, hat

with the propeller
on it—confetti

& kiss me
I'm kazoo for you

fool, counting
down the days

like those numbers
before films, a glimpse

that once, before Abbott
& Costello

a screen test
lady winked & was

gone—spliced in,
us laughing.

GUTBUCKET

I want, like
water, you—

something wet
gainst the back

of my throat. Carry
me out

reel me in
I been down

this well too long—

FIELD SONG

The narrow hollow
of her spine, lying fallow

CHEER

I am
a stadium!

your cheerleader
sans underwear

half–
time lover

back door man
leave your

little porch light on

BLUE MOVIE

It's midnight
midday once

we draw shades
like movie screens

to make love, the light

shining through
in slivers—

It's Paris, it's Egypt,
it's Utah that summer

we drove out, the heat
a blanket we kept

tossing off us
or trying to—

Inside
we sweat another skin—

bed a barnyard filled
with strange, double-

backed beasts—
his pussy

on her chin, her cock
in him—

confused, crowing
dawn as noon sun

streams in—

JOOK

You have me
to you quite addicted

dear—my hands
in your mouth—

my wet-
nurse, succor,

cure. That old
booze

of you's
what I want—

dry gin, new
world, Old Crow.

SUMMER SONG

I think of your kiss
& bite my lip. Place

your hands into
upon my wounds

Hell & heal me
with your blesséd body!

I shake like a booty,
I thieve, and grieve.

———————

You are some sort
of September

I look for your red
car everywhere.

O Summer! O Rider
in your blue skirt

greening across the plain!
An autumn inkling

———————

Lift myself from bed
a body still

lying there, outlined.
O where tonight

be your weight?
My hands miss the way

they's lighted upon
your back bare

A murder of crows
flock of black

birds, heavy
hanging the trees.

———————

I dream of grief.
Madame

le Panache
penning her long

libel about me—
guilty. Sudden

awake I believe—in
your arms rise

like water—
laughing we scare

scatter the birds away
Their long south journey

OVERTURE

When I have begun the long
unraveling that is autumn

When my hands grow
still, without rings

When the moon looms
close as a midnight

beach in summer
& I want to run

my hands through it
just bury myself

Then, loving, you smooth
my eyebrows down

& my eyes roam, alone
drift along the street

already buying you flowers
frail, fragrant weeks

JITTERBUG

Today nothing
sounds good

to eat—not ribs—
not veggie

burgers nor meat
& twos (though

the cobbler in Normaltown
Cafe might do).

I drive past pickup
windows, unordered—

only want to chew
your fingers like a child do—

to taste, watch
with each bite

—a breath—your
body & breastses grow

as if my mouth led
to your smooth stomach.

Darling, it is
your darkness

where I want
my body to be

buried. You burn me
at both ends, send

the geese bumping
within my skin.

EARLY BLUES

Once I ordered a pair of shoes
But they never came.

FANTASIA

Day disappears
  like a dove
into the dark

of the magician's hat—
  abracadabra
alakazaam—my hands

flutter about,
  offstage, lost under
night's false door.

———————

The stars a school
  of fish just
beyond reach

flitting beneath
  dark water.
I hunger.

———————

Night knocks
  like a policeman
The moon

that nosy neighbor
        peers through blinds
into our room.

————————

My life like a limb
        I've crawled out on—
found myself

asleep, tightroping, don't
        look down—

dusk a clown car
        the stars keep climbing
out of, till we can't believe

there's more. There's more.

————————

Hangnail moon
        tugging me
like crazy. Go way

————————

Dark dreams.
    Swimming.
The cough

of a radiator
    coming on—
drowns in its own

small water.
    Gonging on,
along.

————

Each morning the blind
    man's gauze
unwraps, lifts off

and he can see!
    dawn's steady miracle,
you asleep beside me.

AUBADE

There is little else
I love: the small

of yr back, your thick
bottom

lip stuck out.
Your moue makes

me wheeze & want.
Wake. I am like

that big Bessie,
a red cow's plea—

milk me, baby.
Will you stay?

Or rise, as sun
does, & make us day?

BLACKBOTTOM

Like coffee
I do not care

how bad you miss
me—strong, black, I think

of you, head
aching or is

it heart—each
morning me wishing

you boiling, steamed
with want, then

saying ah, awake, after.

NONES

Stammer me.
Stutter utter

in my mouth
my name. Soon

midday & I will again
see you—a lengthening

shadow. A late
noon knelling

kneeling. Boo,
it's you I mutter

mumble, you
I curse croon—

BOOGALOO

And so you say
something

to me like a silence

Which I will kiss
Which my face will press

against, and muss
yr makeup up

Your bordeaux dress

uncorked, let's
breathe awhile

We will shake till
we are again still

Till our loud

lateness wakes
our nosy neighbors

And the dog, listless,
lays down with

that thud you love,
sighing.

MIC CHECK

This morning I wake
early & crave

to call you & whisper
dirty ditties

into your ear—
to put my mouth

to the receiver & hear
you pant & want. The wide

shifting sands
of my hotel bed

a desert, bleached expanse—
days too hot, cold

all night. Phone cord
like a lure

& I caught
on land, can't

hardly breathe. Much
less move.

Your mouth parts
& my name

comes out. What
I want—mussed sheets

of music—the faint
buzz of distance—

this thirst—your voice—
thronging

my tongue.

TUNE

In the Africa
of your eyes—my

lost tribe—
I am safari

this stumbling
shooting off

foolishly. Apologies—
you are no country

Hottentot to trot

you are not. Nor
hunter great am I

though I the sea
for you would cross—

Forgive me—
your ivory etcetera

I have smuggled through
customs

into tuneless this

CAN-CAN

I am some sitcom

star—too old
to be acting

this a-way—
You lay me

out, ко—
Okay,

they say, is an
African

word—I now
know how

a lexicon can
become less, turn

to mere mutters & other
words for *yes*—

BOASTS

Wouldn't be no fig leaf
if I was Adam

but a palm tree.

————————

Once I danced all
night, till dawn

& I—who never
did get along—

decided to call a truce—
my body

buckets lighter,
we shook hands

& called it blues.

————————

Mama, I'm the man
   with the most

biggest feet—
   when I step out

my door to walk the dog
    round the block

I'm done.

SONG OF SMOKE

To watch you walk
cross the room in your black

corduroys is to see
civilization start—

the *wish-*
whish-whisk

of your strut is flint
striking rock—the spark

of a length of cord
rubbed till

smoke starts—you stir
me like coal

and for days smoulder.
I am no more

a Boy Scout and, besides,
could never

put you out—you
keep me on

all day like an iron, out
of habit—

you threaten, brick-
house, to burn

all this down. You leave me
only a chimney.

SWING

You climb the tree
of me—limbs,

knots, your name
carved right

above the heart. And every
year another ring

discovered around my middle
like a moon!

A planet distant. A redwood.
Into my crook you set

yourself a spell
and sing.

Shudder me my thousand
leaves, brushed

by billion winds.

STRIDE PIANO

I wish to tell you I want
you to come down

where kudzu takes you all
a sudden, the light,

the porches bloom
(& are no stoops) with bourbon

& even the talk has a song

long since gone.
In your cold country

the maples don't even try
keeping their leaves.

Am I a sap for saying
so, for wasting a tree

with what you may never hear?

Hold me, dear,
beneath the pines, their

leaves of wire
that storm & sing & will not

let go this green—

PRELUDE

The red ink of insects
killed covers everything

Woodchucks grown
bold, emerge behind

the woodpile, sniff
round the porch

Sweet mama, honey,
even the bees insist

at my door, why won't you
come in & sting

The red hint of insects
killed staining evening

ERRATA

Baby, give me just
one more hiss

We must lake it fast
morever

I want to cold you
in my harms

& never get lo

I live you so much
it perts!

Baby, jive me gust
one more bliss

Whisper your
neat nothings in my near

Can we hock each other
one tore mime?

All light wrong?

Baby, give me just
one more briss

My won & homely

You wake me meek
in the needs

Mill you larry me?

Baby, hive me just
one more guess

With this sing
I'll thee shed

NOCTURNE

I have other names
for you—sin, cobalt

blue, whatever fits
& is not too French.

Forget. Foaming
the mouth, I bark

out commands, cat-
calls. Wolf-tickets—

I call you Paris,
Telemachus, whatever

that means. I mean
sweet hijacker, you make me

want to make you
mine, to kidnap

ourselves & fall
in love with our

captors. My kisses
the prayers a hostage

makes—holy, please,
begging be saved.

★

★

2

You are the beautiful half
        Of a golden hurt.

{ **Gwendolyn Brooks** }

BREAK

I'm about to waltz
on outta here—your hands

cannot stop me
nor your noisy

nudity—
O the brass of your body!

sliding, trombone-
style—bop doo bop

blow! No more
decrescendo, *mi amor*

mi morena, we'll rhumba
bongo maraca—

baby, don't go!

CANTATA

Pulling mad toms
by their mouths

from the river, one
after another, the thrash

& fight still
in them, their prickling

whiskers. Such
is catfish

trouble: raining dogs
& meows, put out

my pail & catch
only mice. So like this,

love—the stinging
struggling in one hand

in other the reel
the line, to which it & I

are tied.

{ A R I A }

She is rainy season
She is a freezing

She be the reason
I am before you singing

She is treason
She pleases

the eye Glory
be Goodness me

She sets
afire me

I am obsolete
Discontinued are we

She is penitence
a dear distance

{ CHORUS }

She walking
away like being

pulled—
by an unseen

force, a dog
perhaps. You know

the joke—walking
an invisible mutt,

the stiff leash—*hardy
har*—muzzle empty

as a gun. This wasn't
like that. She teetering

tall in heels
like Achilles

{ D U E T }

This town is twos—
all split—a blues

club with no black
folk in it

except its tophat
mascot—& me—

        Each street
christened twice—

a President becomes
Prince—

        the highways
called too many

names. We are all
natives

        where I live
things too long stay—

                    the train
whose tracks I must cross

to sleep, calls out mid-
night, then stalls. Mist.

We are each this
crossroads—the church

with its new name
& bldg & lit-up sign—

both sides begging Make Sure
Whats Worth Living

Is Worth Dyin For
beside the Alpha

Omega fraternity.
My mailbox stays

empty, home only
to hornets. This town

                    is twos—
& tain't nothing—without you.

BLUES

Gimme some fruit
Gimme some fruit
Fresh salted melon
maybe some mango too

You had me eating pork ribs
You had me eatin ham
You had me so I was feedin
straight out your hand

Gimme some fruit, baby
Gimme some fru–uit
Something red
& juicy I can sink
these teeths into

You had me eating peas Lord
You had me eatin spam
(You had me so turned round)
I never dreamt all you said
came straight out a can

Gimme some fruit
Gimme some fru–uit
Gimme something strong girl
to clear my system a you

You served me up
like chicken

You deviled me like ham
Alls the while I never knew
you had you another man

Gimme some fruit, girl
Gimme some tomato too
What else is a poor
carnivore like me
without you supposed to do

JIVE

Do you remember the heat
lightning? Great

sheets of it south
sudden—your mouth

making mine water,
thunderous, this air

accent-thick—
so car sick

I weaved the road
home. Pulled over

the police offered me
2 choices—their bright

lights making me
mole—see

the inside
of jail, or forget

all about you.
How I have grown used

to the dark! Once
I did not dare

whisper, utter your
name—but here, in flashes

of light I am unafraid. You
you you I says

& mean it! Confess
nothing. Make me

a deal, backroom, bail—

RHAPSODY

Tonite too many things lead
to those white

rooms the face makes
once skin pulls back

—what's beneath the black—

Lord, teach
me how to return

to that thing called
flesh, how to give up

this ghost—

The woman I woke
to the world with

gone from the places
once we stood. The floods,

rains, nothing falls

on this land—These nights
sky seems closer than home

same way I couldn't see here
there. Some days I wish myself

a different shaped heart, made
round to fit like a watch or a glass

eye, something I could take out
at night & polish off—shine—nothing

beaten, or held blind in the gut.
When I wake

it is with a taste

dry like wine in the mouth
Each day an onion, raw

& watery—an eye—
Love, send me

to sleep like an arm
like a night watchman

SORROW SONG

Saying goodbye to the body
her body, to what

we knew or growed
used to—

on the subway
home, her mouth still

on my mouth
like the gospel

(thick as a cough
or its syrup) hummed

by a woman on the loud
orange seat beside me.

What else besides us
is this? working

down bone, a bright
hymn—asking, asking.

VESPERS

Along this strange shore
I am alone with only

the cruelty of song—
night's chant is

around us, or me—
the hum of her

gone. Alone even
God is no good—

no hymn can take her
off my hands, pressed, kneel-

ed here in front
of this altar television—

flickering—finally
even sleep has left

me stranded, unbottled,
flotsam swaying wind.

PLAYER PIANO

On the sun-starched
deck of a fishing boat

I have watched fish flip-flop

helpless as a heart—
thwap-thwap, thwap-

thump—and wished
to be caught

just like that,
a keeper. Mouth

that won't quit moving—

Afternoons I wander aisle
after aisle in the bookstore, leafing

through women's magazines
to see if my name

lists among diseases
on slick pages marked Your Health,

How to Spot a Cheat,
the latest from Spain.

Please quit lying

to someone else, save all
your stories for me—

This afternoon I tore out
cards for perfume

grew lightheaded

and thought of you—overwhelmed
yet drawn near, the way bees

can smell fear—then smeared
competing scents

over the thin
skin inside my wrists.

Don't mind the cheating
I mind the leaving—

For days I've felt
sick. My stomach

a-swim, a ship
tossing. Think

of you two together
and the day I will pop in

to pick up whatever
I left: unlit

candles, underwear
folded neat and bleached

white as a flag of peace.
Driving home,

feel the quease of days,
my car's lingering reek

till I reach under
and find the offender—

under my seat, out of sight—

an apple, uneaten except
by time and heat. The rest

forgot, wrapped in rot. Soon
I'll teach my hands

better, how to roll over
to beg—

For now, chucking that husk
away, I think of stones

thrown into the sea,
how still

for you I would churn
its salt to taffy.

HARVEST SONG

Lover you leave me
autumn, tilling, a man

tending his yard,
or one not even

his own. Outskirts
of town a farmer

one-armed, walks his fields
into fire—my neighbor

on his knees with a razor
trims his lawn. Next door

I am in the pines—
grass thirsting, and up

to here in weeds—
poison, neglect,

I have tried to forget—
nothing works. Let

the birds rabbits
termites have the run

of the place, the worms,
I will take them in

FOXTROT

Yours is sweet
sadness, bitter after.

Mine numb-
ing, then regret.

I hope again
to touch your feet—

REED SONG

What any god
    would, to hold
you, do:

    Hands round
the neck of you
        I blew
breaths into your mouth
hoping some
    sounds would come out:

You, the barest blue

———

Believed, I did,
    I could
save somehow you:

You who had swayed
as the tallest
    grasses will
then silent
    fell into deep reeds

In me, everything sank

———

I have heard
               tell
of men who sing
        for snakes, slow

who can make even death
bow

     ————————

What once a world was
was now
             only this
faint music
made by the moon:

    Your eyelids grown thick

The world, loud, I could not
rescue you into

     ————————

When I look too long
at rivers
          you are there

Your tightening hair

It is then I pick up my horn
play again your name

to whomever, ever, will hear

———————

Do not board
that train beyond:

———————

Stay hereabouts

while I hold
you, speaking breath
        kissing your woodwind mouth:

    Dusk gathers
    around us like a crowd

till I can, no more, sing out

COUNTRY (& WESTERN)

This is the letter
I never meant

to send, rural route
one, a chart

to what's forgot—
a chant or revival

meeting—a warbling.
Yo de lay hee—

the mailman empty-
handed arrives. Attempted

not known.
I am lonely as God

must be & for all the world
cannot sleep—

Lady Lucyfer,
listen—

you in your frozen
under, banish'd

it is thee I rebuke—

I am at your door
step, un-

hinged—ash at
my feet—yodeling—

You the devil
come to take me

away? or some
angel who fell I'll

never tell

RIFF

I am all itch,
total, since you done

been gone—zero
sum, empty set—

counting. Calculated.
Abacus am me—

a shell skin
game, Georgiaed

grift. Follow
the bouncing

ball! Guess—
I am gross

profits, no net—
And from some great height

(as if in a tech-
nicolor cartoon,

late night, where the heart
up & leaves its chest)

comes crashing
crushing down

blue from the sky: a safe !

BLUEGRASS

No use driving
like rain, past

where you at—
where—

yet here
I again am, id-

ling, radio catching
some song

like an eye, barely—
will you, toward

tomorrow, turn
once more? Solo I am

somewheres west
chasing drinks, ghost

limbs, cyclones

DISASTER MOVIE THEME MUSIC

Winding back roads
I believe in you

Winding muddy back roads
I say I believe in you

Wheels got stuck baby
What good's belief do

————

Train in my way
Can't hardly cross

Train in the road babe
I couldn't hardly cross

By the time I got
to mom'n thems

Heard tell you
were a-ready lost

————

Cyclone hit and
tore my town apart

Cyclone hit town
Tore us clear apart

O how that swift
freight train sound

made off with my heart

_____

Standing at your back door
The dogs bark so loud

Knocking on your back door
Till your dog barks so loud

As many times I come here girl
Now I'm not allowed?

_____

Creek done risen
Creek done rose

It ain't the creek that
took off all them clothes

_____

Lightning struck me once girl
Thunder sounded twice

Lightning struck me once now
Thunder hollered twice

Caught you in the kitchen, huh
Sipping cold red wine

———————

Doctor told me wait son
Your heart it's beating faint

Doctor told me wait now
My thick heart beating faint

When I saw you kissing on him
You thought I'd be fit

and tied—I ain't

———————

So when it is you hear me
shutting your screen door

So when you hear me banging
shut your sweet screen door

Don't expect to see my
brown behind no more

————————

Walking toward the pickup
head inside my heart

Walking toward my Ford
echo inside my heart

Keep on turning clutch
and key

Won't hardly start

MADRIGAL

Who can stand
spring? The weeping

willows drooping
The azaleas bright

The bow-legged beauties

who walk me into frenzy
All this returning

My eyes burning

Road windstrewn with limbs
severed like Roman statues

I am not brave
like the dogwood shade

Pray, soon autumn
will come, undress the trees

DRUM TALK

I cannot bear to become
something far-off

from you—sound,
extinct star, constellation

of bone—I was
once here

you will say,
fondly, even—

My face among
such dark I cannot

face—grace
is overrated.

Lord knows I am myself
unsure & alone—wreckt—

ship, rocket
stranded, snared, stripped—

I am both the naked
& the priest we parade

past—boiled
alive. Such skin, well-

seasoned, rare,
I hope once more

—with yours—to share!

CALYPSO

I touch my hair and
sigh.

You sail
by with your hands

of silk.
(Your fingers always

were worms.)
O the stinging

of the bees!
O the far-flung

morning, a moon
still among it!

———————

Why do you keep washing
ashore here? bottled

up words, abandoned
unsaids

we could start a fire with.
Say it: We must

forget. On my island
at least I know this

(the low, struggling
shrubs, such bitter

tea the leaves make
each afternoon)

& things do not move.

———————

Evening
tide takes my words

away, help spelled
in sand. If only

something besides
sun should see me!

My arms weak
from waving. So far

away the ships
see not my smoke

think it not speech.
By moon I write

not to be seen
but to keep sane—

always the sound of sea.
Unhand me, old blue!

———————

Rescued. The island
a world—it's the world

returned to which tinies,
retreats its entreaties.

Even the dogs
here do not know me.

O battered moon!
is it true you

shine the same here
as there—that some plants

only for you awaken? Tonight,
landlocked, walking far

from any harbor
into my mouth salt blooms!

GUMBO

How the stomach, starved,
spits out food—

ballooned—is how
I love you. Too

much. And all
over Africa the locusts

move in, un-
invited, and eat

up everythang.
Dear, I needs

a benefit
concert! Some star

stud affair. Send
food soon—

this regime
must end. Child,

I have left only
skin—an old

unstirred soup's—

ENCORE

Are the proper
authorities notified

you're aloose—

heartbreaker like you
should be outlaw

on the run—I am
myself a man

most un-wanted, profile
in your local post office

a lost puppy
love. Girl, it's criminal

how you treats me—
the time I'm doing

be hard-
hearted, no one

phones, none to write to.
O Maestro

take it away—
drumroll please—watch

me whiles I flee

LOCOMOTIVE SONGS

We were hobos every year.
It was cheap—

Our mother each
Halloween smudged our cheeks

stuffed us in someone
else's clothes—

We hopped houses
like trains

asking for sweets

Much like last night,
empty-armed, at your door

I begged you

———————

Tonight the train horn
sounds like plenty

enough loud
to warm even the autumn—

The night air with a nip
that catches by surprise—

White light, blue
light, fog starting to rise

—————

She has me tied,
a tongue, to the tracks

Her new man's
elaborate moustache

Train comin fast

Can't cry
out to save my life

Drats

—————

I've heard tell
of a town where the train

bound for New Orleans slows
just enough, a turn

that folks place cars
good only for insurance in—

The train cashes them
coming round the bend—too late

to stop, to slow to derail—
That's how I feel

watching you & the station
being pulled away, one hand

hovering the emergency brake
the other

out to wave

AUTUMN SONG

Even a dog got him
a house.

      Me, I am rent

unpaid, or late—
I am a small bird

beneath a big wheel.
Snail-brown

of November. Night.

      Even a bird-dog knows
      what way is home.

Me, I hunted
the high places, the low

where only the wingless go.

      Of the trees, nests
      are all that's left—

in wind pine limbs creak
like an old man's,

a door opening.
The noise beneath my feet!

    Even a bird,
      a dog, got him a cage

he can bark
all night in, or sing.

BUSKING

The day folds up like money
if you're lucky. Mostly

sun a cold coin
drumming into the blue

of a guitar case. Close
up & head home.

Half-hundred times I wanted
to hock these six strings

or hack, if I could, my axe
into firewood. That blaze

never lasts.
I've begged myself hoarse

sung streetcorner
& subway over a train's blast

through stale air & trash.
You've seen me, brushed past—

my strings screech
& light up like a third rail—

Mornings, I am fed by flies,
strangers, sunrise.

DOO WOP

Honey baby
Lady lovely

Milk shake your
money maker

Shoo wah
Shoo wah

Countryfied
Sudden fried

Alabama
mamma jamma

Low bass
Fast pace

Past face
Femme postale

Penned pal
My gal

Corner song
Done wronged

BANJO

And after 3 days rain
the frog song stops

—which had womped
& bumped loud like a distant

chained-up dog—
and the birds

begin—mockingbird,
wren. *O Susanna*

don't you cry fo me—
an unthumbed string

of days, dis-
cord. A few toads lie

splat in the road & find
I am counting blessings I

never before spoke.
Down the sky comes

grows the grass up—

I plead with you
—the nerve!—to start

again your whispered
name—let

them frogs gossip on
all night—if they want—

FUNK

It finally forms—the stank
of days without you,

unwashed & unwanted
hours. This whistling

I at last can place
my lips around. *Wah,*

wah—guitar
riffs, rips open

my heart's tourniquet
—a prison stint

without conjugal
visits. No chance parole—

what the devil am I
without you to do?

Back-
sliding, off-bass,

shaking hands with Satan.
Get a grip! this

is such slight cross-
roads to bear

left on, to lurch
& lunge. Girl, you still send

me to moon, to Seas
of Vapors, Crises,

Ingenuity, Lake of Dreams—

SLEEPWALKING PSALMS

Verde que te quiero verde.

{ Lorca }

(1)

Every day since I have practiced a sort
of amnesia, forgetting keys, misplaced
names. I have begun to escort
spiders out of doors, into wind, unrest

reaching them at last. Even then
you rise up, remembered—a polaroid
or slip of paper where your writing's begun
to fade. Black, turned brown. I try to avoid

spring, but dust rises and settles over
all things, even the words like
ours, *his* and *hers*, who stole the covers
all seem so far. Green again. Schwinn bike

in the garage I'll never ride, three-speed,
its thick chain locked. You gone with the key.

(2)

The television we bought tides me
to sleep. My alarm radio cannot find
stations outside of town, only night
and tinny music of overpaid teens.

Who won? Each night I fall
before the final buzzer and never
quite know. I drift. It's my call,
one I can't quite make—over

my dead body, your girlfriends say.
I understand why they love you enough
to hate me. I hate me too—pay
too much for bad service and tough

sirloins, overtipping waitresses who
don't call me hon. They work for you too.

(3)

Soon I'll thank you for leaving
all at once, and for good—
no more months of begging,
or not, of waiting for what

we both know only grows,
goes away—our nights days
we'd lie beside the other awake,
pretending sleep, sorrow

a child snoring between us, slightly,
child we'll never have. Thank you
then, for not even the note, just my
opening the door to find you

missing, like my fortune cookie
our now-final meal, broke open empty.

(4)

Sometimes I feel like the stargazers
I bought you (and you left behind
to die, and remind) will last forever or
at least one week longer. Petals find

the table, but most linger and scent.
By phone I talk a friend down from the ledge
of his latest love; my mother in New
York, a city she once feared, now

visits solo, taking in a show. Parent
to my parents, I've seen them grow old,
apart. I think of dropping aspirin
in the drunken mouth of the vase to hold

them upright—instead, neglect the stems,
let the water stand, and still they bloom.

(5)

When I said I didn't mind
your leaving I lied—
even the funny-lookingest kid
in class gets a valentine

and I hear he's now got mine.
These nights I've become
caged by quiet, a zoo of one—
a polar bear pacing like tide

his half-empty pool, loopy from heat,
coat grown green—or some lust-
lost captive who won't quite mate,
so his keeper brings in a stud to save

the breed. Or so, unkept, you claim.
Tell me his name.

(6)

Stumbling home in last night's
smoke-soaked hair and clothes,
strip bars all closed
and wanting to call you right

away, to plead and preen.
I try sleep instead. The phone
can't even recall your voice, no
more your name on my machine.

Lord, let me never drink booze
at least for one more week.
Lord, let me eat more fruit
than comes in a mixed drink.

No one answers
where you are.

(7)

There are no more saints—
only people with pain
who want someone to blame.
Or praise.

I am one of them, of course.
Miracle, or martyr, or worse—
wanting a desert to crawl
out into, marking my fall

by sun and thirst
instead of by this silence
that swims over me. Oasis
not really there, penitence—

you the sand I've crawled across,
my hairshirt, my tiny albatross.

(8)

I love you the way a liar loves
lies: because they grace the mouth,
because I know nothing else. Because.
Each night the light grows later,

a little, and is useless—no more
can I see you. Though sometimes my car
detours your darkened house
to see if your car, foreign, sleeps alone.

I never stay to hear your dog whine
goodbye—or, worse, face a forgetful bark.
Home, I stay awake long as I can,
want sleep to hold me tight like
an electric fence in rain. No luck—
my neighbor's noisy light, restless dark.

(9)

Barbeque dreams: I sweat and turn
on the couch like a slab grown burnt.
Wake to the vagaries of smoke and still
daylight out. Something about a will

I won't write, something about a pill
you forget to take. The cat
that came to visit after we split
sleeps steady, stretches his back.

He won't come when I call
but won't leave either—meows, rises
and scratches along the pole
of my porch, daring me to try

and pet him, or not to try.
Or is he a she? Maybe.

(10)

These days so hot you forget
water, you forget to eat
or breathe, all you want
is for the sun to stop, yet

it won't. Nor the grass.
Still, even the heat won't last,
darkness filling us, my eyes
grown wide and watery. *Allergies,*

I lie. I try forgetting you,
then pretend, then don't have to
as much anymore. I can even see,
stand, our favorite late-night TV.

Soon leaves fall away with baseball teams
and even I will lose your name, not sleep.

CHORALE

Quite difficult, belief.
Quite terrible, faith

that the night, again,
will nominate

you a running mate—
that we are of the elect

& have not yet
found out. That the tide

still might toss us up
another—what eyes

& stars, what teeth!
such arms, alive—

someone we will, all
night, keep. Not

just these spiders
that skitter & cobweb,

share my shivering bed.

TORCH SONG

The heaven of her
hips—over me, such sway—

She got some saint
standing at the gate

keeping the crowds away.
I would get down

on knees, or pay
to build a stain-glass mission

if that would get me in—
I'd slave

& scrub & sing
in Sunday best till I was clean

as a broke-leg dog—

I'd save & spring
for a whole new church wing

if that would let me see
my Lady of Fog

& the Forty
Sorrows again—

FISH STORY

For you I would give up
God—repeal

once & for all, unkneel—
you are beautiful,

little devil—redboned
rusted.
        I trust

you take my soul
someplace I don't want

to know—
dance me round

till dawn. I sleep
long & wake with a crick

running down my neck

to remind
me a you—find

my top drawers empty
my eyes watery

& wind & when
will you again—

To repent I wander
down to the forgetful river

—wait for you there—
& wonder

if the uncaught, low–
down fish know

how lucky they are

JUBILEE

Sister, you are a late-night
preacher, laying hands

upon me cross

a tee-vee screen—
I bow down & send you

all my green—
trace my palm's outline

so you can bless me
rich. You can go & abscond

with my mission's

millions—or take way
the collection plate

that doubles
as my hat through rain.

Woman, knock me down,
out, anoint—

just don't leave me lone

like God
done, promising return.

SUITE

No more flights—
the climb up the steep

steps to your roost
I will

no more make.
Delirious, this.

A dizziness—
spell I'm under, looking

up, like a skirt—
am far from your fire

detector which sang
unceasing, whenever

you cooked. Smoke. Thin
I have grown

like your walls
—but no more

will I hear, no—
your neighbors' breakfast

of spite. Lady, it may
have even been hell,

but it was ours
& warm. I am down

in the furnace, or out
along the reefs—

I have carried lugged
to the top the kerosene

have lit the light-
house & left—

3

I am at the gate of a lost life;
I am at the door of my own harmony.

{ **Jay Wright** }

ENVOY

I quit. Resigned
from your company

entirely—I walk
like paper. Short

notice. Mama,
boss lady, I'ma

miss you—so too
the trees. Time

now to get down
to brass, to this

bidness—of breathing—

SCHERZO

Such schism
of sky—the light

the comet falling
like a second
coming

––––––––

An answering
An afterlife
  of light

––––––––

Our upward flight
from this land
it's an Egypt—a slave

who wings sky
rising

––––––––

  A wind which
we are in

––––––––

On your left
out the window
    look:

————————

The lights of
the city lay down
—a dying man

————————

Night's thick shroud etc.

————————

A sudden calm came
thinking of the day

when the plane
will burst

into bloom—too ripe—
its plumage

will plummet
will hold again earth

————————

A brightness above
the storm clouds

———————

Pity, them
that have not

(yet) touched
your face—

each kiss
a thing I could

not claim—
Duty Free

———————

The praying that lands
this plane—still—afraid

———————

God knows how
long I have leapt

awake, afraid, without you—
now, far from

your fingers
& perfect pitch

I cannot help but
say I'm still

unstill—alive. Decide
I will sit, say

grace & wait out
the dawn, keep

the dark company—

RAMBLE

Lady, you are my Mobile,
Alabama—lowdown & too hot

for human habitat—
you are good

to be a long
ways away from—

Sure, I never been there
but I hears

things, the damndest
things—say

some powder road leads
away & never

looks back—I thank
the stars' luck

& think of you
as Exodus, a Migration

Great—I'd rather
work, I would, sleep standing up

than wake with my head
cradled by your hips

in a town chock full of fools
who own

only their shoes—
than be buried behind

some stubborn
mule called morning

ANTHEM

God, you are gorgeous—
& gone—

left no trace
among the trees

that line this lawn—
rain-fed

& -worn. I am warning
myself—take

no prisoners, hold on
not at all—

yet even without
a guard the chain gang

breaks rocks out
of habit—*hunh*—does not

look up to see
one man—*hunh*—chains

trailing—*hunh*—broken
as the jailbird's

wing, fleeing the field—
back stripes—*hunh*—stars

TACIT

Even language
leaves us—even the train

traveling fog
ends—hot foot

powder all round
my bed—the ants

who my house invaded
heading everywhere, hungry

for what is not there.

Since you, honey,
my cupboards being bare.

I off the army quickly
unlike a child

who holds her magnifying glass
above the hill, picking

& waiting—patient—till sight
spirits into flame

HONKY TONK

At least
I do not need

a comb
to run you out

my system,
my hair—nervous

central circular.
This town's not near

big enough, baby—
one saloon, a strip

club & this buzzard
of a cop who keeps

circling circling
And still

this traffic

SAXOPHONE SOLO

Drive till sun stares
me down. Radio & the cicadas

with their static wings—
I am singing

to myself again.
The way we don't know

the world spins until

we try standing still—
The way clouds swirl

& purple, the not
cool evening.

The dog in the flatbed
in front of me, surfing

delighted, tonguing
heavy air—

The way he does not bother
with death (or vice

versa), or the fall
possible ahead—a broken hip

then off to sleep—

Instead he is wind,
what makes his ears bend.

SLIDE GUITAR

Tonight I wake with mud
in my head, a thick

brown I sink
my line into. Fists

full of fish.
Tonight even the storm

cannot calm me.

My hands tonight scatter
about the place, folded

quiet like fine lady's gloves.
Cue the saddish music—

how like flies it rises!

Outside, the suicides
float by buoyant

in their lead balloons.

PLAINSONG

The green is gone.
You can walk & walk

looking for a clearing
& never find one.

Instead the woods around
you, breeze.

And memory, which lies
down with history

as you do, among stone
& whatever's fallen

to watch the sky wind past.
Which it does—

the clouds above
do not think & do not

think, therefore, of you.
You don't mind

the getting lost.
Or loss. The tip

of an ash tree starting red—
business end of a slender cigarette.

LYRE

Walking up the hill
from hell, singing

the shadows back—
all them wanting

to be among the living—
at my pants

leg like cockleburrs
or children, the dead

clutched clung

———————

I carried you cross
the coldest reaches

Led you back from that
under I had placed you,

hurt by my hand—what
I couldn't take—

the way I had wounded,
yet went on

When I said I would
not turn to look

I lied. The lyre
in me is strong

enough even the birds
the dead can hear, but how

could I make you? I wanted
at my hand you

listening—instead you
hesitated, wished

to follow
me. Indeed. Now

I know I was merely
barking

at the least noise, that by
a leash you let me

———————

Love, it was not that
my back was bare

to you—though it was
that too—nor to see

that face of yours
I already by heart knew—No,

I turned cause dust was
what made me up

& I wanted to see some
of the salt of you—to lick

whatever had helped you not
fall apart when far

forever from me you went

REQUIEM

Your name is harm.
The bar fills

& empties eddies
like a drink & is not

the answer. Ain't—
I'm all kinds

of lost, watered,
down. The shot

glass like
a microscope strong.

I should be a natn'l
day of mourning

one week minus
mail. Entire month

of Sunday—a sabbath
swaying

mouthing hymns—
Where, pray

tell, went the words?
Rider, you are a whole

church-worth of hurt—

DIRGE

Rain then. Things
could not get worser—

go on, murder
me. Take

your hands which have
no hurt in them—

such blameless beauty—
& throat me through

& thru. Turn me into
a thing dumped

alongside the road,
dear, shot in heat

of moment. My scent
the dogs barely will be

able to detect—infrared,
night scope, that's how

they'll find me—hiding—a hoax,
prank, recanted—gone

from wronged to put-on—
from speculation, headline,

to a page 8 correction,
a retraction none reads

nor believes.

DEEP SONG

Belief is what
buries us—that

& the belief in belief—
No longer

do I trust liltlessness
—leeward

is the world's
way—Go on

plunge in
—the lungs will

let us float.
Joy is the mile-

high ledge
the leap—a breath

above the lip of the abandoned
quarry—belief

the dark the deep.

EVENSONG

At dusk women
walking alone give off

the strangest light—
till you realize they're not—

a dark dog races
to meet one, leash

tailing; or,
a boyfriend not worth

the wait, gleeful
ungraceful, follows

far too close.
Children tire of ignoring

their mothers who half-watch
them holler. The boys

skateboarding beyond
even their bodies

have got it right—

fling yourselves, friends,
into whatever guardrail or concrete

the world has, then find
someone to get it all

down on tape.
Later, the falls will

seem obvious, about
to happen—re-wound,

the women all look
better off—and those

who fall shall stay

airborne, oblivious, halfway
to happy.

OPERA

Why do we talk
to pain? I am like

a man motorcycling
into midair—dusk—

tossed & broken
by a car—glass singing—

who cusses
the silence that after

an accident settles.

Later they will find
a headlight

& handlebar deep
in the dash—

But right after flying
& flipping

the driver the bird, we reach
out apology, a hand

to shake with whoever
hurt us, bowing, thanks

for helping slow us down

SONG OF SOWING

We are always
always saying

goodbye—the fare,
well, it's expensive

the train leaving—
and with it, winter

which winds up
underground,

awaits. Beneath
our feet answer

leaves we failed
last fall to sweep—

springtime full
of cardinals—nightfall

sounding a train's far-away
whistle. Once

asleep
it all, for us, quits

mattering—or is us—

ROCK

I swing shut.
Spit, & am a shame.

I get drunk on little
things, pissed, swear

her off like sweets.
The rocking chair don't

by itself rock—
If only she

was here to tell me
shut up, quit

complaining, to kiss
my mouth closed.

INTERLUDE

I know now who
I am writing this to

& it ain't you

Afraid it's me
I cannot leave

alone well enough—

a sparrow striking again
again his own reflection

& ROLL

My teeth it seems
won't quit coming in

late like teenage
children. Nights I pace

myself asleep.
My dreams stark

easy to explain & she
not among them.

O Despair! why
now has pain left me

alone, to blame, without
even ache to help explain!

Like a bird I swallow
the smallest stones.

MOOD

I got the 'noid
more'n old

Staggerlee—me,
I shaken

hands with the void—
Please to meet you.

Betrayal'll
make you shoot

soon as see.
A shadow boxing

me in, this killing
feeling—

season of pigeon
extinct. It is late

enough perhaps to want
my old life back

or none at all—
Times like this should

outlaw what's unsaid.
And up

in the mind there
a burner

half-cocked, triggers
over, again, its dry fire—

Mercy, baby,
take hold a me!

INSTRUMENTAL

I have put down words in order
to again breathe——have set aside

my horn to hear,
inside, the pounding——

the loud foundry, its anvil——
long ignored. John Henry

got nothing on me!
cut down all the limbs

around me, cleared forests——
have fought fires by setting

others of my own. Let
these pages slowly curl

& catch——soon,
I will pick again up

my axe & ax God
to let its song be

plain——a green
undergrown place——

PASTORALE

Outside azaleas bloom loud
& red like ambulances

rushing to save someone
or least try. Bees tend

to the eddying leaves.
Roadside, pine limbs

still litter the lawns
after last month's icestorm

axed them down.

———————

Lights out—
we navigate

the colding house,
feel for matchbooks

which you save
to bring light, I

to remember where
I been. Wax brings

a light which lasts—
which we wonder

why not always.

———————

By April the camellias
have let go

lie in a halfhearted halo
around the bush I never

trim, though always
think of before sleep

as if past
loves, that drifting—

Day brings a beauty
unbidden—rain, a bee

building flowers
with its wings—

what I never
noticed till the endless

rain that indeed ends.

_____

Ice turns even
the trees heavy

& helpless, all
morning falling—

a song of breaking—
winter & plunder.

I wonder we're next

_____

If there's a way
to save the sick trees

which in my yard sway

I don't know.
One day they lie

prone across the drive
where I find them dressed

in vines, or ice,
or ivy that grows

full foot a day.

———————

Afternoon & no thaw—
cold still covers the pines

snapping them in half.
Only the oak still stands.

We go out & drag
the limbs & trunks

out of the slick drive
like a drunken uncle, awkward,

carried home smelling
of Christmas—

cursing the needles & branches
we sweep.

———————

We know spring because
the roads fill

with men waving
us on, urging slow

& yellow—
the police call

for pledges & the hedges
overgrow. We give

what we don't have—

time & these trees
that don't ask

but bloom anyway.

————————

A weathervane
offering wind and N E W S

————————

No ghost— just the voice
of a radio, surging

back on—flashing
midnight—singing again

with the rest of the lights—

like the night I awakened
to the tune of a cat trapped

under the house, whine
coming up the vents, echoing

my every step.

Tomorrow who will see
that cat slink out

into daylight, walking fresh ice,
or frost, or a yard

wet with weeds?

—————————

And time like a train
I hopped on a while

back—did not know
it went one way only—

Whistles taking us where

—————————

Two bees both
flying & falling

hover together
in our way while we walk

the steep street
to the station—one adult

fare, one-way—please—
the coach all exhaust

its sigh & mine.

Home—your stray
hair a surprise

found clinging to my sink,
my blue bed—

your traces faint
as the neighbor cat's footsteps

cross the hood
of my car, yellow

pollen prints that even rain
won't erase.

————————

Those six deer
who crowd my yard

will not scare
for anything—they stare

at me as if I am the stranger
& they are

right—but then
there are more

deer than ever
round here, gathering grass

or dust & blood beside
the road. We are

neighbors, at best
natives, of a world

cold then hot, always
about to

fall apart. But not.
The half-dozen

turn, paired,
& slowly step into,

among, the fallen trees.

————————

To praise this place
To praise

the sawdust trace
a carpenter bee makes

burrowing my back porch
To praise the lurch

forward, into days
lengthened

then leaving—
To praise the unseen

face of the paper boy
who, still sleeping, delivers

the day, throws what all
this town knows

onto ice, or fireant
hills, onto lawns

struggling green.

VOWS

My wife of words,
ambassador of grief.

From you I am far,
firefly fading, jarred.

Across the night lawn
lightning bugs wed.

Through woods echoes
my widowed voice.

MUZAK

When old, do not let me bark
at passersby—let me be

like the slow motion, down-
the-street dog, ignoring

the cardinals, the colors
he cannot see, even us

as we tiptoe by—
Friend, please save me

from being the neighbors'
fool hound who woofs loud

at every grey squirrel, stray
noise, or lab rushing past

to meet some lady—from being
that cur who cannot help but howl

all night like newlyweds
keeping the world awake. O terrible

angel of the elevator, the plane,
insufferable unquiet we pray to, afraid—

Please make me mild

HERO

We are making that noise
of ourselves once more—

again we burn,
lighting the fires

& realizing we can.

From this mortal shore
we set out

candles for the lost—
our house

of light. Do not forget

the wine. Do not
forget the time

when it was all
we could do

not to. Have I fallen

into the machines
of happiness

again, the turning that
can only mean

well? The boat barely
bows down with dead

weight: a soul
slows us so little.

O the tides of this sandy,
unsanctioned life. Tread light.

Some nights I have felt
a sort of happy. Others

the flies
fleeing my body.

Tonight I feel fatal

as sleep,
as apple.

SONG OF SOLSTICE

So this is what death sounds: screech
of tire & twist, smoke

around & swerve
from the deer now rear-viewed, scampered

into the pines. Smell
of paper mill.

Almost. One day
the doctor will say sorry,

that's it, nothing more
we can do & sorrowed you'll walk the long

way from hospital home—no way
home at all. But now, for no good

reason, I drive with stars
heavy above, thick

on my face, the stink
& sky all around. *Almost*—

not now, driven well
past signs that tell

where exactly we are, what town—
till we reach places where trees cease

becoming anything else, grow tall.

CODA

The stars, they don't do
anything—their silence

lights this smoke
of sky, then sputters,

burns out. Night
forgives nothing.

No longer do
I love you—faint

comet, far-off fever—

nor whisper
into my hands

mouth your name—
I have folded instead

my sorrows like a winter
garment—moth-filled

unwashed—I will
no more wear

PARLOR SONG

        I spider the days—
each one a shorter

stitch in the quilt
which you will kick off the bed

quickly, when you return.
Dawn—

patchwork once—
is now these scraps

all day I save & make
something out of

that the dark undoes.

     ————

        You & your travels!
your encyclopedias

have kept me keeping

company with the quiet.
Outside

my window the suitors circle, smoke

their unfiltereds
into ash. They ask

after me.
They serenade,

guitars in hand, play
their second

fiddle. After you
they ask also

      interested
Are you dead—

Have I any word—

      I repeat—
You have taken afield

your samples to sell & soon
we'll see you scraping your boots

along this very stoop.

———————

The dog, greying, has grown

too tired to hunt
the underbrush, to rise

& whine whenever
the wind our screen

door creaks.
              At night I dream

your skin quicksand,
ground that gives

way—sinks—

        I wake alone.
Come home
        & warm

your side of the wrought
iron bed

I've kept for you cool.

————————

        For you my list of things
to fix will be nil

though the old place you will

barely know—it's too much
the same as that day

you whistled out our door
with your nicotine

promises & schemes
of green.

      Our old photos
fading, the piano

unplayed, your fingerprints
cover the mirrors

as does dust. All night
I toss

like the scattered stars you steer
somewhere by, shore

to shore, hawking your
insurance
      & whiskey.

INTERMEZZO

Lately I head down
to the river

& watch what washes
past: garbage

boats, tugs, occasional
sail. Dangle

my legs over the side
like a lure.

Unlocked, bicyclists
wind past on paths

only they can follow—
& you, somewhere, smart

in your new hat,
dressing for Saturday night—

Never again that shade
of lipstick will I taste

nor leave the jalousies
open to let in air

& our neighbors' envious stares.
Speedboats cough

along, the river heads
on relentless, regretless—

the way only the sea
& gravity may meet—

You descend the long
flickering stair

into what light is left—
still bright enough to blind

me, ashore, as sun skips
like stones off the steady water.

THRENODY

Even cars have their graveyards,
piled and turning

the one color
of after—

And me with nowhere
to send my bones

to be counted,
made whole.

This is
Providence, Providence—

Not even a dentist to visit
once a year like an aunt

squeezing my cheeks
too tight.

Without you I got no one
to say *sorry* to—

Only this winter
pretending spring, fooling

few blooms. *New
Haven, next*—

The trees never do reach
our train that clatters past

blurring cars—three parts
primer, the rest rust—

the color of ash,
of ember.

COTILLION

Tonight I am a man
tap-dancing the train tracks

red light—red—
while the 10:50 nears,

sweet horn blowing.
I jitterbug,

Charleston bound—
take down

the tarnished stars, my breath
will shine them up new.

Tonight I want a tongue
stuck to the wintry track

& swear when that freight train comes
I'll yank my thick head back.

Tonight I'll grab hold
the striped arm

of the crossing bar—
let it dance me

round real slow.

Tonight I tango
alone.

LATE BLUES

If
       I die,
let me

be buried
       standing—
I never lied

to anyone,
       or down—
wouldn't want

to start up now.

LITANY

The dirt grows up
around us, dear,
the dank & the way down

of it. The day.
Once I was
in love. Once I would not say

or could not, the under
that awaits.
Today, I say over

your one name,
sound
that sole gravity.

———

The old draw-
bridge, rusted, is always up

———

North, New
London—we cross
ourselves & the river

into the past—
the submarine
memorial for those lost

at sea, sunk
miles under—the docks dry—
the rust & mist

———————

Count me among the missing

———————

The apples
have not kept

their promises,
grown rotten

& ran, skins
bled into brown

———————

I come to your town
fog clinging to bridges
to the baring branches

———————

In the calamitous city
in the songs & sinners
among the thousand throngs

I barter & belong. Out
of the coward's tooth
& arms of ocean

out of sheer
contrariness
I continue. Keep watch.

      ————————

Hunger has me
by the belly

      ————————

Why does the waiting
scare you & me
the silence that surrounds

it, us, this life—

I am inside this
stone you call
a city. I am king

of the gypsies.

Thin throne air.
No crown to speak of.
My body

dying, divine.

————————

The day will, I know,
come—not now—
but soon & they will say

you are gone

Will I know it by
the lack of breath
—mine—the long grief
in the trees

Or will it be you
they tell of me—sickened,
stiffened, through.
Do not

worry. Will be
me beside the foot
of your bed, nothing

haunting, just
a hint. A wish.
Think

of me & breathe!
say over
again my many

my million names.

ELEGY, NIAGARA FALLS

for Bert King, d. 1996

Here snow starts
but does not
stick—stay—

is not enough
to cover
the bare thaw-

ed ground.
Grief is the god
that gets us—

good—in the end—
Here—churches
let out

early—in time
to catch the lunch
special—at my local

hotel. Sunday—
even the bus
boy has your

face. And still
having heard
some days later you

were dead—
I haven't caught
sight—day

or night—
of the Falls. I know
they are somewhere—

near—like you—all
gravity & fresh water
& grace rushing through—

A NOTE ABOUT THE AUTHOR

Kevin Young's first book, *Most Way Home,* was selected for the National Poetry Series and won the Zacharis First Book Award from *Ploughshares.* His second book of poems, *To Repel Ghosts,* a "double album" based on the work of the late artist Jean-Michel Basquiat, was a finalist for the James Laughlin Prize from the Academy of American Poets. Young's poetry and essays have appeared in *The New Yorker, The Paris Review, The Kenyon Review,* and *Callaloo* and have been featured on National Public Radio's *All Things Considered.* He is editor of the anthology *Giant Steps: The New Generation of African American Writers* and the forthcoming Everyman's Library Pocket Poet anthology *Blues Poems.* A former Stegner Fellow in Poetry at Stanford University, Young is currently Ruth Lilly Professor of Poetry at Indiana University.

A NOTE ABOUT THE TYPE

This book was set in a version of the well-known Monotype face Bembo. This letter was cut for the celebrated Venetian printer Aldus Manutius by Francesco Griffo, and first used in Pietro Cardinal Bembo's *De Aetna* of 1495. The companion italic is an adaptation of the chancery script type designed by the calligrapher and printer Lodovico degli Arrighi.

Composed by Stratford Publishing Services, Brattleboro, Vermont
Printed and bound by R. R. Donnelley & Sons, Harrisonburg, Virginia
Designed by Gabriele Wilson